They

*For Ann —
And her wonderful
poems.*

Sue Ellen Thompson

They

Sue Ellen Thompson

Turning Point

Published by Turning Point
P.O. Box 541106
Cincinnati, OH 45254-1106

ISBN: 9781625490988
LCCN: 2014946894

Poetry Editor: Kevin Walzer
Business Editor: Lori Jareo

Visit us on the web at
http://turningpointbooks.com

Cover art:
Katherine White
Katherine White Artography
Frisco, North Carolina

For my father, Elliott Axel Thompson (1920-2012)
and for my child, Thomasin Parnes

Acknowledgments

Comstock Review: "I Dream About My Father at 87"

Delaware Poetry Review: "My Father at 84"

Delmarva Review: "The Silent Dinners," "After the Houseguests Leave," "A Burst Pipe in Maryland"

Fledgling Rag: "A Birthday Gift," "Braiding the Foliage," "In Philadelphia," "Envy"

Free State Review: "Falling on Ice," "For Sale," "Dinner at the Oxford Firehouse," "At 89, My Father Takes Up Swearing"

Freshwater: "Home," "A Surprise," "July 17"

Gargoyle: "The Paper Dress"

Hoot and Hare Review: "The Gift"

Nimrod: "Echo Rock"

Poet Lore: "Inheritance"

Tar River Poetry: "2002"

Table of Contents

I. Wolf Watch

A Photograph of My Daughter at 9

She's sitting in a dining room chair.
Light through the blinds has tightened
its straps across her narrow body
and a blow dryer has transformed
her wispy hair into a child-sized helmet.
Her legs are crossed and shackled
to each other at the ankle, and she grips
the chair arms with the wild-eyed stare
of one who is about to undertake a journey
full of risk and turbulence instead of a simple meal.

A Name

I had the book of names, the Jennifers and Emilys,
but knew she would be none of these.

The names my friends were hoarding
for their daughters—Meghan, Courtney,

Ashley, Sage—seemed out of date
and somehow inappropriate.

How could I know my child would be
something I'd not yet heard of, never seen?

Not Speaking

In 1970, for almost a year, I stopped speaking
to my mother. All she could see
were the children I'd bear, their hair
rusted Brillo, their skin the color
her fingers had turned when she minwaxed
the dining room table. I had been dating this man
for only three months and she was convinced I'd end up
living with him in a dingy Brooklyn apartment.
Standing there, in the phone booth I shared
with a dorm full of women, its close-fitting air
of Kotex and socks, listening to her
as she pleaded and wept, I knew that this
was our last conversation, that she had said all
she could think of to say and that nothing
she'd say now could sway me.

Forty years later, my mother is gone,
and I have a daughter who isn't at all
what I thought I'd received when the nurse
handed me my package. But when
she bites off her words to me,
I will not go to that place where I sent
my own mother—where she didn't know
what was happening, that it had already happened
without her and could not be undone.

The Silent Dinners

My mother would sit down last, having told
the six of us to start without her. My father,
gazing at his plate in disappointment, would say
that he had ordered this same dish
for lunch today at the local diner. Who knew
what insults she'd endured, or why her patience

had worked its way to the end of its long tether?
She would slap the placemat hard, and before her tears
could frighten us, storm off to her bedroom.
My father's head would be in his hands,
ignoring her strict rule about elbows on the table.
He'd take a bite—as if that might inspire us

to carry on in the absence of our leader—
before losing faith in the charade and following her
upstairs. Who knew what forgiveness meant,
or if it could even be dispensed by one
so clearly injured? Who knew what went on
up there, or if they would appear again

that evening? We would eat as we had been
instructed to, our eyes cast studiously
downward. No tormenting the younger ones,
no jockeying for seconds—as if rehearsing
for the night, some forty-odd years later,
when our mother, who had borne the insults

of disease all summer, finally lost patience.
She thrashed, she moaned, she sat up,
lay down, cried out *Lord, don't make me suffer.*
Then she marched off to her grave, while our father,
head in hands for what seemed years,
sighed long and hard and followed.

After the Houseguests Leave

I unmake the guest room bed and let
the washing machine twist the sheets
into heavy coils of dampness. I erase
all evidence of breakfast, scour the sink,
and sweep the drive clear of the leaves
that twirled so frantically in the wake
of their departure. Pressing memories
of dinner from the table cloth, I think

of how it was before they came—
the house a vault of quiet on a quiet street—
and before that, of the summer day
I found my mother twisted in a sheet,
wondering why her fever had come back to visit.
There was an even earlier day:
I was a guest in my parents' house,

before I came to stay. Rising from her chair
at dinner, my mother pressed one hand
to the vault beneath her ribcage. The leaves
of unease stirred in me. The day before,
I'd dozed beneath a dome of trees, listening
as the quickening breeze of a neighbor's child
twirled among the ghosts of laundry.

Anniversary

November 15, 1979

That morning, to ease my nerves
before the town hall ceremony, I went
for a run in the park. From the top
of the hill, near the Greenwich Observatory,
I could see Tower Bridge rising
from the sludge-colored pavement
of the Thames. The concrete sky
behind it and the path on which I ran
sent the truth reverberating
up the stanchion of my spine.
I had an envelope in my pocket,
with a check for the doctor whose hand
had pressed down hard on my belly,
my life about to change.

*

November 15, 2006

I meet my husband at a restaurant
to celebrate. Instead, he hands me
a letter, in which our now-grown
daughter lays it all out: four pages,
single-spaced, of things we've managed
not to talk about. Each year
in mid-November, I think
of that restaurant. Of the meal
that was not eaten, the glasses

that were not raised. Of that letter,
whose secrets would require
that we begin from birth again
to know our only child.

Home

The place your parents brought you straight
from the hospital, where you spent
those endless years of grade-
school. Or maybe it's the place
where you raised your own
children, where you were never alone.
The place you retreat to after the divorce,
or when circumstances force
you to go there. According to Frost,
they have to—but you know the rest.

Who can say for how many weeks
after moving you will lie awake,
staring at the clock-radio, before
you stop listening for the pre-dawn roar
of traffic down your former street—
before the word begins to rise from deep
inside somewhere as you approach
the yellow blinker at Main and Oak,
which, like the porch light your mother
flicked off and on when you and your first lover
were parked at the darkest edge of the lawn,
reminds you where you belong.

Moving Out

All those dresses that her mother bought
are tossed upon the growing mountain of debris:
Leaving home is easier than she thought.

The little wooden lobster boat she got
in Maine goes down without a eulogy,
along with the other gifts her mother bought.

Her childhood is over; the lessons that it taught
seem distant now and meaningless as history.
Leaving home is easier than she thought.

Smoke from the teenage battles that she fought
mingles with the talcum of her infancy
in the soft folds of the dress her mother bought

for a school dance. It hangs there like an afterthought,
its underarms stained dark with irony.
Leaving home is easier than she thought.

A final trip upstairs and she is off,
kicking aside the birch's skirt of leaves
as if it were a dress her mother bought.
Leaving home is easier than she thought.

For Sale

Few buyers came to look, and when they did,
what could they see? Not the twin bed
where my daughter begged for my embrace
each night as darkness dropped between us,
or the lantern wavering in the dogwood tree
over our quiet picnic dinners after she'd
gone off to college. Not the sun-wracked
sofa where every afternoon I napped
in the lush company of my own desires,
or the desk to which I brought an acolyte's
gratitude each morning for the god
who'd let me in without a proper job.

The realtor flung and flapped her arms,
hurling her superlatives around the rooms—
for who could sell, except the rhapsodist,
the empty frame for so much happiness?

The Empty House

House that we bought just a month before
we were married; after the wedding, the rooms
unfolded anew. House where I brought

the baby straight from the hospital, sat
at the dining room table, unbuttoned my blouse.
House of the Christmas Eve dinners,

my niece and her boyfriend together
on the piano bench, which to this day
bears a mark from the heat of their thighs.

House of the homework assignments, the three of us
up half the night making two-inch-tall teepees
of bark from the birch tree and little plaid bedrolls

cut from an old flannel shirt. House
so toxic with anger, a teenager's
venomous mouth, that for three years

we dared not have anyone over for dinner.
Then, when she left us for college,
a silence so vast

we inflicted our surplus endearments
on a long-suffering 12-year-old cat.
House of near-human sounds—

bone-creaks and moaning, sighing and wailing
in storms. House of our long years of marriage,
your limbs entwined around mine

like ivy around the round stones
of the stone walls surrounding the yard.
House of the woodpile, the woodshed,

the canvas wood carrier carried
six times a day from the shed
to the wood stove, the smell of felled maple

and oak. House I came home to
after my mother died, put down
my suitcase and lay on the bed

with my coat still on, hands
folded over the knot of my sorrow
as sleep closed its massive green door.

My Father at 84

A muted keening. A wandering back and forth.
A slippery grip on where and when.
Alone in his ten rooms up north.

He cannot taste. He cannot hear
much of what the television says.
Now, it seems, he can no longer bear

Christmas, which reminds him of the days
when he was father to five and led us in,
blindfolded, to the tree. Or Memorial Day,

which brings back The War. Since
my mother died, he's become
another man entirely: submissive,

prone to weeping. I know that some
fathers get cantankerous when they're old
and sometimes I wish he were one

of them. I can look at my child and know
where she came from. But when I look
at my father I think, *Where did he go?*

A Surprise

You couldn't set foot in my mother's world
without the proper bra. Which is how I found
myself, on a Saturday in 1964, trapped
in the lingerie department at J. M. Towne's.

Watching from a knothole in the curtains
of the dressing room, she instructed me to "bend"
at the waist and "pour" myself in. The cups
filled rapidly, and if I didn't straighten

up before they spilled, she'd make me try
a larger size. So you can see why
it troubled me when my daughter came home
in her twenties and her breasts were gone.

She wore a green plaid shirt that stretched
across the featureless farmland of her chest.
In her laundry bag, a white elastic vest,
designed to press the contours from her flesh.

How would she survive without the earthworks,
firmly molded and secured with lace,
on which the generations had relied?
How had she managed to escape her mother's eyes?

Postcards

Postmarked Ann Arbor, Fort Wayne,
Memphis, and a dozen other places
I never knew she'd visited,
my daughter's postcards
to her widowed grandfather
were the only way I had of finding out
what she was up to during those years
when her phone calls thinned
to almost nothing. He would leave them
on the nightstand in the bedroom
where I slept when I was visiting,
and I would read them—row
after row of minuscule block letters
pausing patiently before the fenced-off plot
she'd set aside for sheltering his name
and address—just before I went to sleep.
She often signed them, "Thinking
of you, Pop," and I did not for one minute
doubt which shelf he occupied
in the library of her affections.

"And how did that make you,
her mother, feel?" a shrink
would no doubt ask, and I
would have to answer
that it made me happy—happier,
I think, than if those cards had been addressed
to me. Here was a man who'd waited
19 years for a grandson, who had kept
his wishes silent as six granddaughters

were born. Here was a man
who liked to spend a summer day

fishing lazily along the Merrimack,
winter weekends stacking cordwood,
and here was a child who wanted to be
at his side, doing what he did. They seemed
to have an understanding: she would give him
all the love that she could spare
for generations preceding her own
and in return, he'd never say a word
about her tattoos or her piercings
or her boyish haircut, or ask her why
she hid her breasts and let
her mustache show. He would simply think
of her as the grandson he'd been waiting for,
and she would always think of him
as the man she wanted to be like
when she was old and had
no grandson of her own.

Cross-Dressing

When they're staying in the house alone,
my daughter and her new friend, Stephanie,
decide that they will dress like us and take
a photograph. Standing together in my closet,
they choose a linen skirt from Talbot's,
a stiff white blouse and low-heeled pumps.
Stephanie puts on my amber beads
and matching earrings and,
because she's never met me, stands
before my bathroom mirror wondering
what kind of woman, wearing such things,
produces a child like Thomasin—

who stands before her father's mirror,
fine hair parted neatly on one side,
khakis and a hound's-tooth jacket,
blue shirt and a maritime museum tie
with tiny ships in tight formation.
She poses, hand on Stephanie's
substantial thigh, on our front porch,
camera propped up on the railing
as our neighbors walk, bewildered, by.

When I see the photograph, the shock
comes not from how much clothes betray
the woman I've become, but from
how little she has changed since someone
took that photograph of the three of us
leaving the hospital, and a stranger,

who just happened to be walking by,
said how much she was like her father.

At St. Paul's School for Girls

Like a girl—arms crossed against
her chest, not about to let
herself be dragged off to young
womanhood—but like a boy,
with her splayed-knee slouch
and fitted cap of hair:

a teacher brought her to me,
wanted us to talk.

I chattered aimlessly
about myself and poetry until
it came to me: here was
my child at seventeen,
estranged from her own kind.

But I was not
her mother, and she
was not my child.

So we just sat there,
looking at each other
miserably, waiting
for the years to pass, so she
could go to college, graduate
and find a small community
of peers who would accept

what she'd become. So I
could have a grown child

who'd come back to me,
arms tattooed and outstretched.

Postcard: Lakota Wolf Preserve, Columbia, NJ

Hey Pop! I went on a 24-hour getaway
with some friends to the Delaware Water Gap,
two hours north of Philly. We floated down
the river in tubes all afternoon, camped
for the night, then got up early
for the "wolf watch" at a place nearby
where 25 timber, tundra, and arctic wolves
now live. There were bobcats, who'd been someone's pets,
and two red foxes. All were either born
in captivity or rescued from roadside attractions,
so they weren't afraid of humans. I was thinking
about that cougar you once spotted
in New Hampshire. Next time you see him,
tell him there's a home for him here in New Jersey—
isn't that where you spent your "wild youth"?
I miss our early morning walks. Love, Thomasin.

II. Flood Zone

The Gift

I choose the window seat so I can see
the plowed brown fields of eastern Maryland
give way to snow and icy streets
as we approach New Hampshire.

A handsome, younger man from Texas
takes the aisle seat, and of course I'm at the age
where flirting, much like décolletage,
no longer flatters. But once the plane

inclines its nose to sniff the possibilities
of thinner air, this bronzed god leans
across the empty seat to ask,
"What is that you're reading?"

His attention is a gift I've learned
not to expect, but here it comes,
as startling as a San Antonio snowstorm
and as welcome as the April sun

in New Hampshire. The burdens of the week ahead—
cleaning out my father's freezer,
putting clean sheets on his bed
and trying to convince him he'd be better off

living near me—dissolve in the golden
radiance of row 15, making me believe
that I can keep my father in his home
and safe until the moment

that he passes into my mother's keeping,
and that I can face my own death
with the steady gaze she leveled at the window
just before she died, as if she already

knew what it was like for the birds that flew
up to the blazing rafters of the autumn sky
and for the horses in the field across the street,
grazing their way steadily out of sight.

I Dream About My Father at 87

Someone has given me a horse,
for which I am certain I have not asked.
Its steaming muzzle makes me want
to hold the long bone of its head
in my arms, but the skittishness of its hooves—
it seems to be standing on only three—
inspires a mild terror. Clearly
it is mine now; it lowers
its forelock modestly and picks
at some threads in the earth.

In the agate of its eye
is the curve of my own worried face.
I have no halter to lead it home,
no pasture in which it can graze.
And yet it follows me, shoes ticking
across the frozen ground. How
will I care for a horse in winter?
What if it slips and breaks its leg?
What will I do if it dies before spring
and I have no hole prepared for its grave?

Postcard: Laurel Hill Cemetery

Hey Pop! Things have been good
here in Philly. I've been exploring
Laurel Hill, where six Titanic passengers
are buried and where there is
a "Millionaire's Row" that's like
a little city built of mausoleums.
I took some photos of the lettering
that's carved into the stone and rode
my bike the whole way home along
the Schuylkill River. How different
everything looks now that the leaves
are gone. I'm thinking of you
and the six-month winter you are facing.
I'll find a way to visit soon. Love, Thomasin.

A Moose

A moose by the road in the moonlight,
dark grass trailing from his teeth.
Tall, awkward animal—part horse,
part cow, part high school geek—
he gives me a withering look,
like the one my daughter cast at me
when, shocked to see
that she no longer tweezed
her brows or plucked the dark fuzz
from her upper lip, I asked
what she was telling me.
He turns his furred flank quite deliberately
and goes on eating.

I Take My Father Out for Dinner

At seven, I was wearing my first
figure skates, afraid of the teeth that bit
into the ice, although my father claimed
that they would give me traction.
But when I tried to pull him—
young enough, back then, to sit
cross-legged on my sled—across
the frozen lake, my feet slipped out
from under me, and I bit the ice hard

with my chin. Tonight, I set my feet
and knees squarely beneath me as I bend
to help him out of the passenger seat. I put
my arm beneath his arm and raise him up
to standing. Although I know that I must bear
his weight across the frozen parking lot,
it almost seems that we could skate, arm
in arm, off to his favorite restaurant.

Falling Through

After I've lost an hour's sleep
for every obstacle in my father's path;
after I've pictured his tinder bones
going up in a puff as he trips on the rug
or collapsing into the sack of his clothes,
this happens:
              He plops himself down
in his favorite rocker, only to have the seat—
a delicate network of decades-old cane—
disintegrate. His frail body folds up,
knees to his chin, arms flailing
and failing to hold him.
                 He becomes
a purse, its clasp snapped shut,
its contents hidden and roiling.
He becomes what he was
when he started out: his mother's
favorite, clutched by and clutching her arm.

In Philadelphia

There's dark fur curled above her sock
and a shadow on her upper lip.
She's let her eyebrows grow back in
and she's cut her own hair so it hangs
in painted strands across her forehead.
But as we're walking down the street,
she lets my steps fall in
with hers. Emboldened then,
I swing my arm around and let
it settle lightly on her shoulders.
Joy like a torrent rushes in,
for here I am in Philadelphia,
on my way to a restaurant
with my 28-year-old child.

Postcard: Ocean City, New Jersey

Hey Pop! It was unbearably hot
and humid in Philly today,
so my housemates and I headed out
to the good old Jersey shore—not far
from where you said you used to take
your station wagon full of kids
when they were young. We picnicked,
swam, and napped all afternoon.
Then, at sunset, we shared a bucket
of curly fries and watched a bunch
of little girls rehearsing for a dance recital
in the theater on the boardwalk. So many
chubby legs in shiny pants and tutus!
So many sparkly eyelids and fake ponytails!
So many stage moms! It made me think
of my rich New Jersey heritage—and that,
of course, means you. Love, Thomasin.

A Birthday Gift

There was a children's clothing store in town,
and when I took her there to buy
an outfit for her second birthday, she walked
right past the dresses I pulled off the rack,
their small yokes choked with smocking,
and with the single-minded grace
of the athlete she'd become, went straight
to a pair of gray wool knickers.

Charmed by this display
of independence at such an age,
I picked out a navy hair-ribbon,
which my daughter promptly wore
around her pale neck, knotted like a tie.

The Gender Spectrum

When my daughter was a toddler, we
would rake dry autumn leaves into a pile,
over which we'd throw a flannel sheet.
At naptime, we would fling ourselves
into its fragrant center and fall asleep.

One afternoon, I awoke to find
myself alone. Heart pounding
like a bass line, I cast my eyes
around the yard until I saw
her standing at the far end of the drive,

rocking slowly on her sneakers as a truck
went rushing by. I stole up quickly
behind her, afraid I might disrupt
her youthful balance, and stood there
as relief, bewilderment, and luck

played over me. While I dozed,
she'd made her way to the margin,
looking left and right before renouncing both.
Was this an indication of her cautious nature
or something I should already have known?

Flood Zone

All day it rains—a stubborn, head-down,
adolescent rain. The drainage ditches fill
and disappear, the undulant brick sidewalks,
then the street itself becomes a memory.
Water steals up the gravel driveway
and into the garage, where it soaks
cardboard boxes and threatens the trunk
where my daughter has stored the only evidence
of her childhood she's chosen to salvage.

I open it, wondering if I will find
some long-buried, indisputable sign
of what I failed to recognize when she
was younger—something to help me define
what she is now. I pull out
a few CDs, some photo albums,
and in between these, the miniature pair
of work boots she picked out herself
when she turned five. The flood continues to rise
in me as I gaze out over the broad, flat reach
of this unnamed body of water.

A Burst Pipe in Maryland

People around here don't expect
weather this cold: they allow
the wind to play beneath their houses,
and no one thinks to leave the faucets
dripping. When it comes,
they have already locked
their doors and gone to Florida.

Standing on the sodden shore
of what this morning was my neighbor's lawn,
I think of my mother, who hadn't planned
on dying first, and of my father,
whose silent, invisible grief
cascaded through him until he stood
surrounded by a lake.

Postcard: Hernando DeSoto Bridge, Memphis

Hi Pop! When I'm not working
at the co-op, I've been building
a ten-foot cardboard ear of corn
to carry in West Philly's annual
Peoplehood Parade. My co-workers
have built a giant head of lettuce,
and the message is that everyone
should eat more locally grown veggies.

I know you'll say that when you were
a P.O.W., the only vegetable you ate
was onion grass and here you are,
about to celebrate your 90th birthday.
I'll send you pictures anyway.

This postcard is left over from my trip
to Tennessee. I remember going under
this bridge on a paddleboat
in the pouring rain. I hope
this finds you warm and dry
and free of any aches and pains—
not vegetables. Love, Thomasin.

Hurricane

Those coastal residents determined to ride out
this storm, the weatherman on TV warns,
had better write their names indelibly
upon their forearms. My father thrills
at this report, having spent two years
in a German P.O.W. camp, where he learned
to thrive on the storms that swept in
from the Baltic. Blizzards were his favorite,
until my mother made a widower of him
at the onset of a harsh New England winter.

Still, this warning broadcast on a mild fall day
lifts his spirits in a way unmatched
by all my efforts to cheer him. Hearing
in his voice some of the excitement
of his youth, I'm happy, too,
that there's a Force 5 hurricane coming,
one that promises loss on a scale
none of us can possibly imagine.

III. Unlearning

2002

The year that my mother died, at the end
of a glorious autumn. The year I stopped
wanting to be like my older sister,
who slept with the noise machine on as our mother
lay dying. The year I forgot
how to sleep, how not to lie there alert
to my mother's least stirring, weeks after
that stirring had ceased. The year that I first
took a pill to get through those hours,
after freeing one from its shackle of plastic and foil
to give to my father, who went to bed
fully clothed and lay on top of the covers,
as if an emergency might still be lurking nearby.

It was the year I stopped staying in touch
with old boyfriends, having seen
my father lie down with my mother
and nap the afternoon of her diagnosis,
as if those hours weren't bringing them closer
to anything more than a meal. It was the end,
you might say, of a long American
childhood, which began in the lush green back yard
of the 1950s and ended five decades later—
first in a tumult of ash on a September morning
and then in a last drift of sparks from the trees.

My Father's Accident

Naked from the waist down, lying
on his side, the towel underneath him
drawn between his thighs,
this cannot be the man who leapt
into the sky, was taken prisoner
by the Germans and survived
two years of near starvation
before returning to his bride.

When I find his clothing
in a pile in the bathroom,
I have to think that I've arrived
just at the moment he decides
it's time to bathe and change
for the flight home to my mother,
who will recognize that he has dressed
for the occasion in his suit of light and fire.

Postcard: Germantown, Philadelphia

Hi Pop—This is Grumblethorpe
(which sounds like a name that you
made up!), the historic house museum
that I visited last weekend. Built in 1744,
it's full of beautiful old books and maps,
which you would love. And did you know
that the first American weather records
were kept by Charles Wister, who lived here
and wrote down things like temperature
and rainfall in his diary? The weather forecasters
in Philadelphia still use his records
as a benchmark—the same way you compare
your winter weather to the journals Grammy kept.

A British general was headquartered here
during the Revolutionary War. Wounded
in the Battle of Germantown, he died
in the front parlor—you can see the bloodstains
on the floor! I hope you're feeling better now
and that the doctor's figured out
who put that icepick in your temple.
Hoping I can visit soon. Love, Thomasin.

At 89, My Father Takes Up Swearing

The army must have taught him how,
and then he spent those two-and-a-half years
in a German P.O.W. camp, with all
the other starving men who used
such words to salt the watery gruel

of their existence. But when he came back
to my mother, she would not permit
a "damn" or "hell" or any of those in-vain names
to cross her well-scrubbed doorsill. He never
slipped in the more than 50 years

I listened. But now that she's beneath the lawn
of the cemetery on the other side of town,
he cannot find his fucking cane—the one
that is no goddamned good for anything
because the rubber tip keeps falling

off. Jesus, what a fucking pain
to bend and search for it beneath his bed,
especially when he hits his head
on the open drawer of that bedside
fucking table. He lies there on the threadbare rug

and tries to remember what the hell it was
he lost. My mother, were she still
alive, would flush in anger and cut him off.
But who am I—who have not leapt
from a burning plane or slept in a barracks

whose floorboards must be taken up,
one at a time, for burning when the coal
runs out—to tell my father what to say?
Where the fuck is his goddamned cane?
Shit, man—I have no idea.

The Paper Dress

She never went to high school proms
and showed no interest in boys. But the night
of the Christmas dance, she came downstairs
wearing a paper Lawn 'n Leaf bag
on which she'd painted the curvaceous body
of the woman she had no intention
of becoming, wearing a snug white dress
with bra-straps showing and an inch-wide zipper
running from her cross-hatched cleavage
to her fishnet knees. The teacher
who was chaperoning wouldn't let her in—
although her friends were wearing strapless,
backless, asymmetric hems that clung
discreetly to one ankle before soaring up
the opposite thigh. My daughter bit
down hard on her own anger, looked
the teacher in the eye and slowly, stiffly,
started walking backwards to the door,
her middle finger raised
behind the paper dress's hourglass waist.

Postcard: Vintage Philadelphia

Dear Pop—I had a great time visiting
last week with you and your two sisters—
Anissa and I spent the whole ride home
talking about how much fun it was
hanging out with people in their 80s.
Aunt Ruthie pinched Anissa's arm
and said it felt like it was made
of rubber—guess there aren't too many
young people where she lives—
and Aunt Connie asked if I cut my hair
this way on purpose—she's hilarious.
Anyway, after listening to so many friends'
post-holiday complaints about their cold,
offensive, older relatives, I feel
particularly grateful that I have
such energetic, charming ones!
Stay warm and eat some
vegetables. Love, Thomasin.

Braiding the Foliage

I braided my daughter's hair for school,
back when I thought she'd grow up to be
a girl like any other. She flinched
and ducked and twisted her head
at distractions invisible to me,
forcing me to start over.
Here is the photograph:
smocked blue dress,
short white socks with eyelet trim,
and two blonde lanyards, pencil-thin,
with a wishbone of hair at the end
clamped hard in a bow-shaped barrette.

Since then it's been flattened
by helmets and caps, waxed
into spikes and dyed ink black,
clipped so close on the sides
and back I can see her scalp
shining through. But when
the daffodils start to fade
and I spend the better part of a day
braiding the lank, green foliage,
there she is in my hands again,
her small head pulling away.

Graduation Day at Deerfield Academy

Seated between the parents of Christian Parker Bordeaux
and Joanna Chadwick Flynn, I think of the day in 1995
when we parked in front of the admissions building
for our scheduled interview and tour. Cornstalks,
pumpkins, and chrysanthemums were arrayed
along the granite steps, and girls in tight wool skirts
were hurrying by. "I've seen enough," my daughter said,
refusing to leave the car. So 12 years later,

I don't quite share the proud, anticipatory state
of those on either side of me as I wait for my niece
to appear in her white dress—because I'm thinking
of the girl who turned out not to be a girl
at all, but who even then knew more
than I about the kind of school she'd have to find
if she were going to survive in a world whose riches
stood at rapt attention as those stockinged legs marched by.

Painting the Crib

The trees, almost no longer bare,
laid their dark stripes across the yard.
I had to splay my knees so I could bend
and paint the narrow wooden bars.

Later that evening, I would feel
the first blunt tightenings of what
once would have been called—although
I'd never thought of it as such—

my confinement. But for now,
a low, almost electric thrum
of anticipation and excitement
running from my shoulder to my thumb.

My mother had declared it was a boy,
based on the football shape and elevation
of my body's absurd cantilever. From behind,
according to her frequent observation,

I still looked as girlish—some would say
boyish—as ever. Did it matter?
I hadn't set my heart on anything
beyond a normal child. But years after

my mother was gone, I often thought
about the confidence she'd placed
in her prediction—dispensed with once
pink bows and ribbons decorated

the nursery. She had a habit of being—
at the very least, in retrospect—right,
but in ways that I could not conceive of,
laboring through that endless April night.

They

Reading "About the Artist" at my daughter's first
solo exhibit, I notice that she refers
to herself as "queer"—a once derogatory word
that is now back in vogue. Unversed

in the linguistic proprieties, I read
on, hoping to unearth some clue
as to the exact nature of her gender-identity view
of herself, and this is what I see:

"Their work is characterized by the play
of the familiar and the unfamiliar, made from objects
they have found within a five-block
radius of their apartment." Who is *they*?

Does she have a partner I've not met—
a co-creator I know nothing about?
Because my experience with "coming out"
is limited to a gay friend from college, she sets

me straight: Since neither "he" nor "she"
is accurate, I should refer to her as "they."
Whether or not I'm okay
with this is irrelevant. If I want to see

her more than once a year, I may
as well begin by unlearning the rule
of noun-pronoun agreement. In this school,
I am the student; she, the teacher. *They.*

Echo Rock

When my daughter was young, my father
built a hut for her on Echo Rock,
the granite mound for which the farm
was named and from which, if she faced
the house, she could pitch her name
and have it flung right back. Made
from barn board scraps the weathered gray
that characterized the foreshortened days
of a New Hampshire winter, it had a single
window facing north and a door that she could padlock.

I hear her still, from the clump of underbrush
that kept her refuge and its secrets hidden,
at the end of a day when it appeared
that she had played contentedly alone.
"Thomasin!" she called repeatedly,
as if there were another of her
and it was time now for them both to hurry home.

My Father's Third Manhattan

One and he gets sentimental and wants to talk
about the old days, when we were still
in grade school. Coming home from work at night,
he'd park the Pontiac in the garage and enter
through the basement—past the science project
on the workbench, past the ping-pong table
covered with a sheet tied back at one end
to reveal our sleeping bags and pillows.

Two and he remembers coming up the stairs
and reaching for the door, on the other side of which
I waited for him, ear tuned to his every
homecoming noise. Just as his hand closed
on the doorknob, I would yank it open.
"The only one of my five kids," he says,
eyes filling as he stirs his third,
"who was always there to greet me."

Although more than fifty years
have passed, soon he will be calling me
a *little tyker*, eyes fixed on the cherry
at the bottom of his glass. Why is this
what he remembers of my childhood?
Why is this the story he repeats? Why
have I never told him I was only trying
to scare him, not to make him weep?

Homemade Postcard

Hey Popper–It's been snowy and cold
this week in Philly, but I've been enjoying
the flickering "flames" of my new
plug-in "wood stove." It brings a little
New Hampshire charm to my big city life–
I just come home and flick it on
for instant coziness and ambiance.
Speaking of comforts, I read an article
in the New York Times about some bees
in Brooklyn whose "honey stomachs" turned
bright red and who produced red honey.
It seems that they'd been gathering
their "nectar" at a nearby maraschino
cherry factory. That made me think of you
and your manhattans. You always say
the cherry at the bottom is your favorite part.
Be careful: I don't want your insides
turning red! Remember what the doctor said:
Drink more water. Love, Thomasin.

A Comfort

When she turned six and wouldn't wear
a dress to her own party,

the other mothers smiled knowingly
and said, "She'll come around."

When she was ten and threw away
the valentine a boy had sent,

my mother said, "She's only ten.
She'll come around." At twelve,

she wore her father's flannel shirts
to school. "They call it 'grunge,'"

her teacher said. "She'll come around
when she's a little older."

In high school, there were other girls
who spiked their hair and dyed

it dark magenta, but only mine
wore underwear designed for men

beneath her low-slung cargo pants.
Waiting outside the school one day,

I heard another mother say,
"I know my daughter won't look

like this forever. When she goes
to college, she'll come around." Then

she added, with some embarrassment,
"So will yours." I shook my head.

My daughter had worn camouflage
to nursery school. She came home

from college with piercings in her cartilage.
"Stop worrying," my husband said.

"She'll come around when she has to get
a job." I knew that would make

no difference. She found a place
that hired her just as she was.

"She'll meet a guy and that will be
the end of it"—more than a few

friends told me this. "You
don't know my daughter,"

I said. But cradling myself in bed,
I thought, *She'll come around.*

IV. Drilling

Envy

There was a time when I envied the friend
who came from money, married money. Then
her husband was taken from her. So I trained
my green eye on the friend who divorced
and had a string of lovers—until her daughters,
one by one, married and divorced. For a while,
I wanted to be the friend whose child, a son,
was very nearly perfect, until he hung
himself. So I envied the friend who had just
been given tenure, not to mention one
of poetry's biggest prizes, when
she received her diagnosis. I knew then
I was better off being who I am:
my husband jobless, my daughter a man,
writing my poems for nothing.

Falling on Ice

You're in a hurry, rushing
out the door, just as the January sky

begins to pale. You're looking
at the geese that rise

in a consensus from the river so nearby
and for a moment you, too,

leave the earth and fly.
But as their undersides

pass over you, you
drop the way that blossoms

drop, their momentary
weightlessness turned instantly

to weight when their trajectory's
completed. And all day,

as you hold the wrist you hope
is just a sprain, you're thinking

not about the pain and not
about that moment when your weight

was lifted from you, but of the suddenness
with which the earth reclaimed you—

like the husband who relinquished you
six months ago with your assurances

that he should take the job,
that you'd be fine here on your own.

And now you cannot scrub a pot
or hook your bra without him.

My Father's Laundry

When my mother died, my father discovered
he could not fold a fitted sheet. Patiently,
I showed him the appropriate technique,
but in the months, then years, that followed,
I would find the bottom sheets he'd laundered
spread out on the guest room bed,
where they remained until one
of his three daughters came to visit.

He could operate the washing machine, the dryer,
he could roll a pair of socks until one
disappeared inside the other,
but those fitted sheets defeated him—
or else that bedroom was the place
he went to say, *I can't do this without you.*

Coming into Walmart

Greeted by a woman with a long gray braid,
who looks about as happy to be welcoming me
as I am to be here, I see a table of men—
in their 80s, I would guess—
sharing coffee in the snack bar.
The greenish light, the sporadic blasts
of arctic air that lift their colorless,
thinning hair each time the vast
glass doors slide open—why
have they chosen this
as their gathering place?

I think of my father at that age:
as if gas were still a quarter
a gallon and his eyesight keen
as a fighter pilot's, he'd drive
every day to the Steeplegate Mall
to drink coffee with the other widowers
in a place that wasn't any woman's kitchen.

Between

No longer living in Connecticut,
but with my husband living there again,
I'm always traveling back and forth
and am not entirely in Maryland,

either. I am not ancient yet,
but neither am I young.
I find myself chastising
my father as if he were my son.

My only child is neither son
nor daughter but seems,
at times, she could be both
or neither—leaving me

uncertain what to call her
when speaking to my friends,
whose children now are marrying
and having their own children.

July 17

On a wooden chaise by the water's edge
I dozed and read, dozed and read,
forgetting that my mother was dead,
that my daughter had decided she was a man,
and that I was living apart from my husband.
I was reading a book I'd already read,
which made it easier to put aside,
which made it easier to close my eyes
and dismiss my own misfortunes.

The wind lifted the heads of grasses
bowed by the heat, like forgotten wishes
revived by memory, then left them listless
again. I did the same: One
by one, I summoned my obsessions,
then waved them off. A restless
bee nursed on the clover beneath my feet,
but I let this sweetness elude me.
For hours that seamless afternoon

I drifted, so far from familiar shores,
it was as if I'd fallen overboard
and no one noticed. My reward
was respite from both fear and dread
but also from joy. It was a kind of death,
this sleep: I was a chord
struck once, dissipating in the summer air.
I awoke to my neighbor, in her yard somewhere,
calling, "Shadow! Shadow!" Nothing more.

At the Kitchen Window

Ignoring the tattoos, the piercings, the triangle of hair
shaved off geometrically above each ear,
the elastic waistband of men's underwear
visible above her belt (which cut across her rear

the way my mother's tape measure did
when I was her age and took my measurements),
my father always welcomed visits
from my daughter, which were more frequent

than her visits home. She'd sit with him on the porch
in the evenings, praising his tomatoes, asking questions
about what it was like to be a pilot or a prisoner of war.
He never said anything to anyone

indicating he was bothered by the way she looked—
except that morning when he stood
at the kitchen window, watching as she took
aim, pitching windfall apples into the woods

that fringed his vast, well-cared-for yard,
and said, "If I didn't know differently,
I'd think she was a boy." I poured
some coffee I didn't want or need

into a mug as slowly as I could
and then some milk, and stirred.
I waited for that thought, and the mood
it cast over me, to settle without a word.

Postcard: Chapel Hill, North Carolina

Hi Pop! I'm on a road trip with my friend
Anissa. Yesterday we went
to "Tomatopalooza," a festival
of heirloom tomatoes. Table
after table of them—you could pick one up
and eat it like an apple. I remember
the tomato plants you always grew
in a whiskey barrel on the patio
at Echo Rock—have you planted them
again this year? I can picture you
about to take a bite of the summer's first
BLT. "Nothing like a ripe tomato"—
that's what you always say! I'll call you
when I'm back in Philly. Love, Thomasin.

"I Love Women"

My father said this to the tall, blond ophthalmologist
who greeted him as he was wheeled into the operating room
where she would give him back his vision. He said it to
the caretaker who tucked him in at night, although he told me
privately that she could "stand to lose a few." He said it
to the stranger in the parking lot at Shaw's, whose head
was pulled so far back in her parka hood that she grabbed
his arm and pulled him close, thinking he was her husband.
He even said it to his grown, transgender grandchild,
who laughed and took it all in stride. Less than a week
before he died, as I leaned across his bed to rearrange
the blankets, he hauled his good arm back
and swatted me on the ass—a gesture that must have cost
what little strength he had. "Pop!" I said, in a voice
I hoped would combine the amused surprise
and muted moral outrage that had characterized
my mother's reply each time he grabbed a handful
of her not-so-youthful flesh, "What are you doing?"
He let his head fall back into the pillow's ample lap
as a smile suffused his ancient face. "Sue, you're looking
good," he said. "In fact, you're looking great."

Postcard: Fort Wayne, Indiana

Hey Pop! I drove 12 hours from Philly
with Anissa last week. We passed
a lot of old farms, sheep, and barns collapsing
on themselves, which reminded me
a little of New Hampshire. Now I'm in
Fort Wayne, where I've been to the zoo,
the art museum, and the old fort
after which the city was named.

The weather has been perfect—
I never thought that I could have
so much fun visiting the Midwest,
although the people around here
look at me a little strangely—
it must be the way I cut my hair.
I know you'd tell me to be grateful
that I have some hair to cut! I can't wait
to visit you in Canterbury. Eat
some kale. Love, Thomasin.

Wednesdays

Along with his two surviving sisters, the five of us
divided up the week, so that one of us would call
my father every night at dinnertime. My night
was Wednesday, and after we discussed the weather,
and he expressed amazement that New Hampshire
could have record-breaking rains while Maryland
clung stubbornly to drought, he'd ask if I had spoken
with my daughter lately. I'd say No, that it had been
a month, or that I'd left a message and she hadn't
called me back, and he'd say what a shame that was,
he didn't understand how silence could descend
between a parent and a child. With that, he'd reach
across the kitchen table with his knotted fingers
for her latest postcard, then for his magnifying glass.
I marveled at the torrent of her sentences,
when her communications with me were so sere
and brief. When he was done, I'd say, "I'll talk
to you again next week," to which he responded
cheerfully, right up until the end, "I hope so."

My Daughter Visits Her Grandfather During His Final Illness

He keeps asking me when
is she coming, when
will she be here and I
keep saying she's on her way
from Philadelphia, probably
in Connecticut now, in Manchester,
barely a half-hour away, and

there she is in the door.
He doesn't see what I see:
a girl-boy, woman-man with a sparse
mustache, with a chest made flat,
with thrift-shop pants hanging off
her ass. He sees his grandchild,
who climbs on his bed
and reads him the get-well cards
and newspaper headlines,

spooning egg into his near-
toothless mouth, patting down
the thin hair that the pillow pushed up,
telling him easily and repeatedly
what she hasn't told me in years.

Postcard: Cherry Springs State Park

Hi Pop! This park in central Pennsylvania
is supposed to have the darkest skies
of anywhere in the Eastern U.S.
I am on a camping trip with friends,
and last night we went to a special
"Saturn-viewing." The telescopes
were manned by serious astronomers
whose laser pointers were powerful enough
to be seen against the sky. They aimed them
at some constellations and even pointed out
a few black holes—which don't look
like much, but are exciting to think about.

Today it rained, but we were able to move
into a cabin at a nearby campground.
I've had lots of great bird-sightings
and a close call with a small black bear.
Hope you're enjoying the dark night skies
and the wildness of your surroundings.
I love and miss you, Thomasin.

The Sail Loft

The yellow building across the street
was once the schoolhouse for the village's
black children. The current owners—
a gentle couple with a son
who has yet to find a school
that will accommodate him—
have moved back to Washington,
where they hope to find
a program for the gifted, talented,
and intractable. My father—

who, at 91, can barely recall
the turmoil that surrounded
the raising of five normal children—
would no doubt say, "All that kid needs
is discipline"—something he has often said
in reference to my brother's autistic child.
I haven't told him yet that one
of his granddaughters is now

his grandson. For fifty years,
the second floor was rented
by a black sailmaker, who cut
and stitched and spread his white
shapes on the dark pine boards.
He must have known what they would do
for a skipjack or a log canoe. But who
among us understands how canvas, cut
and rearranged, can carry us beyond the known horizon?

Postcard: The Wissahickon Valley

Dear Pop: I went on a bird walk here,
led by an old man with a hat and jacket
that looked as though he'd grabbed them
off the Shaker pegs by your back door.
He had a photographic memory of every
bird he'd seen in 30 years. He knew
their names, the color of their feathers,
and could even imitate their songs—
it reminded me of how you can remember
every fish you've ever caught—
even the ones that got away.

Another rainy day in Philadelphia.
Sorry you're in so much pain.
Know that you are in my thoughts;
I miss you and Echo Rock.
Love, Thomasin.

The Last Time I Saw My Father

He couldn't sleep, couldn't get comfortable
in the hospital bed we'd brought
into his room, would push a button
and his feet would rise up to the ceiling.
He had no appetite, he was thirsty
but drinking only made him want to pee
and he couldn't do that, either. In the middle
of the night, I found him sitting
with his thin legs dangling
off the bed, pajama bottoms
halfway to his knees, one hand holding
what I didn't want to see, the plastic urinal
tipped over on the table, out of reach.

With sudden clarity, he looked at me
and asked, "Are we drilling today?"
I thought he might be dreaming
about the V.A. dental clinic, where he
had endured six decades of extractions,
root canals, and a series of bridges that never
seemed to work or fit—the legacy
of his stay in a German P.O.W. camp.
But then I realized that it was 1943
and he was back in Lubbock, Texas,
in the Army Air Corps. "No drills today,"
I told him, and this seemed to comfort him.
"Good," he said, and then, "I'm tired,"
closing his eyes as if he knew
that nothing further would be required.

The Morning After a Death

How fierce the robins
how sharp the light's blade
the yard pure aroma
after all-night rain.

The last breath hauled in
like a clothesline—the breeze
about to make off
with its collars, hems, sleeves.

Today you'll wash bedding
and move the old bed
back under the window
where it has stood

since the time before anyone
could be disturbed
by early spring morning
light or birds.

Postcard: Wild Turkeys,
Pocomoke River State Park

Dear Pop: We didn't see any wild
turkeys here, but there were turkey hunters
everywhere. I took an evening walk
to the clearing near our campsite
that reminded me of our "deer walks"
after dinner in New Hampshire—
that same sensation of stepping through
thick grass on a full stomach.
I love places where I can walk alone
at dusk and not be frightened—
hard to come by in the city.

Anyway, I'm sorry to hear
you've been in too much pain
to sleep these past few weeks.
Maybe you should try
thinking about the hunting trips
you used to take when you were young.
I love and miss you, Thomasin.

Inheritance

After the funeral, I told my daughter
she could choose what she wanted
from her grandfather's New Hampshire farmhouse.
She took the yellowed handkerchiefs
with which he'd wiped his brow
when mowing the lawn those thirty summers
after his retirement; a leather belt,
well-worn but stiff from hanging
where he'd abandoned it when nothing
but suspenders could keep his pants
from falling off his ancient hips;
and the pajama bottoms he had worn
for what turned out to be
his last eight days and nights.

As I watched her fold and pack
her small inheritance in a grocery bag,
I asked, "Isn't there something else?"
thinking of a rug or piece of furniture.
She went directly to the small spice chest
that had hung on the wall for fifty years.
Opening each of the miniature drawers
and peering inside, she said, "Just this"
and pulled out a campaign-style button
that said, "I Flew a B-24," which she pinned
to her stocking cap as she boarded the train for home.

Sue Ellen Thompson is the author of four previous books of poetry and the editor of *The Autumn House Anthology of Contemporary American Poetry* (2005). Her work has been included in the *Best American Poetry* series, read on National Public Radio by Garrison Keillor, and featured in U.S. Poet Laureate Ted Kooser's nationally syndicated newspaper column. A graduate of Middlebury College and the Bread Loaf School of English, she was a scholar, fellow, and staff member at The Bread Loaf Writers' Conference for many years. She has taught at Central Connecticut State University, Binghamton University, Wesleyan University, Middlebury, and the University of Delaware. Although she has spent most of her adult life in Connecticut, she moved to the Eastern Shore of Maryland in 2006. Since then she has been a mentor to adult poets and an instructor at The Writer's Center in Bethesda and Annapolis. In 2010, she received the Maryland Author Award from the Maryland Library Association.

CPSIA information can be obtained at www.ICGtesting.com
Printed in the USA
BVOW05s1628030914

364597BV00003B/9/P